THE
UNITED
WAY

THE
UNITED
WAY

The Next Hundred Years

WILLIAM ARAMONY

DONALD I. FINE, INC.
NEW YORK

Library of Congress Catalogue Card Number: 86-46401

ISBN:1-55611-039-1
Manufactured in the United States of American

10 9 8 7 6 5 4 3 2 1

This book is printed on acid free paper. The paper in this book meets the guidelines for permanence and durability of the Committee on Production Guidelines for Book Longevity of the Council on Library Resources.

CONTENTS

CONTENTS

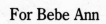

For Bebe Ann

FOREWORD

IN 1966 when I was serving as Secretary of Health, Education and Welfare, President Lyndon B. Johnson sent me on a mission to Miami. The first wave of Cuban refugees, who proved in the long run to be a strength rather than a burden for Miami, were at that time the source of some anxiety for community leaders. It was feared that the refugees would put a greater strain on social services than the community could handle. The federal government could (and did) help, but it was necessary that I understand the dimensions of the problem and that I obtain the cooperation of local leaders in various important matters.

I interviewed all of the top officials and many top business and civic leaders. Almost without exception they said at some point in the conversation, "Have you talked to Bill Aramony?" As head of the Dade County United Way, he did not hold the exalted rank of some that I had interviewed, but he was obviously perceived by all as Community Problem Solver No. 1.

When I finally caught up with him, I discovered why. He not only understood Miami's problem, he understood the federal government's problem, and he had an unshakable conviction that problems were made to be solved.

I suspect that very few people have any idea of the leadership energies needed to keep the United Way going. An experienced leader would be alerted to that reality by the fact that United Way is not one centralized organization but 2200 autonomous organizations, every one of them unique. If nothing more were required than to orchestrate the efforts of such a dispersed collection of unities, the task would be heroic. They say the real test of a leader is the capacity to influence and lead individuals over whom one has no control. If so, Bill Aramony is a leader in the purest sense of the word: He operates under just those circumstances, year after year.

But much more is required than to orchestrate the energies of hundreds of United Way professionals, hundreds of thousands of volunteers and millions of donors. Indeed the very word *orchestrate* is misleading. It suggests that all the players are following the same score!

All organizations function better with some degree of enthusiasm. But there is something very special about the enthusiasm that must permeate an organization committed to raising billions of dollars and upgrading the quality of community life every year through volunteer effort. It can succeed only under a dynamic leader who understands motivation, who has a gift for mobilizing human energies and who comprehends the importance of momentum. A good listener, Aramony absorbs and sorts out the complexities of a problem but is never daunted by those complexities. The reader will find in the pages that follow innumerable signs of his orientation toward the future. He expects new problems; he is forever thinking about the next dilemma that requires attention, the next stage of growth. To him the United Way is a continuously evolving movement. And what it is evolving into is an instrument for community problem solving, a means of breaking down barriers and enabling all elements in a community to work together to meet the most urgent human needs.

—JOHN W. GARDNER
November 1986

The First Hundred Years

The United Way is a century old.

During that time we have undergone a great and elemental metamorphosis. We began a hundred years ago as a useful device (borrowed from England) for a limited purpose—a better way to raise money for certain essential community services.

Now we are becoming something quite different. As we adapt to the massive changes the century forces upon us, we are becoming one of the nation's most important instruments for *building community.*

And the need to build—some would say rebuild—community has become our highest priority as a people.

We are a nation with great and growing resources. But we seem bewildered and demoralized by a great paradox. As our national capacity for problem-solving continues to increase, the agenda of seemingly intractable community problems continues to grow. Our social machinery for identifying problems and for focusing our community energy intelligently on them is not working well. Our boundless collective energy and imagination is not being effectively mobilized and directed.

That is the great challenge of our time.

But I believe that United Way can fill that need. I believe United Way can, and should, help harness to full strength the shared values that we call "community." I don't think we could have done it twenty years ago, or even ten years ago. Now I believe we can.

On our hundredth birthday, we are rethinking the role of United Way in society. We are accepting a new vision of what we are and what we can become. We are learning a new vocabulary. We are learning to see responsibilities and opportunities of a different order.

We can become the instrument through which America rebuilds its battered sense of community.

We can because we are learning to *imagine* that we can.

CHAPTER ONE

Picture This

For decades, everyone knew that no one could run a mile in less than four minutes. Physiologists and athletes agreed that the body could not withstand the effort. It was accepted as fact that there was an impenetrable physical barrier that kept man from running so fast for so great a distance.

Roger Bannister was a medical student. He understood the chemistry of the body. And he saw no medical reason why his body, if conditioned properly, would give out if it ran a mile under four minutes.

Bannister trained hard for the accomplishment, but not thoughtlessly. He trained with an informed conviction that his body could do it.

Bannister ran the mile in 3:59.4 on March 6, 1954. He collapsed at the finish line and was color blind for a short time, but he recovered perfectly. The psychological barrier had been broken forever.

Since then, the mile has been run in less than four minutes thousands of times. Two runners, John Walker

and Steve Scott, have run under four minutes more than 100 times each. As the mile record continues to fall, the vision of what the mind and body can accomplish together is constantly being revised.

Organizations, like people, can never go beyond what they can imagine.

United Way can become the instrument through which America's full capacity for community is restored. But first we will have to imagine that we can.

Imagine this: a United Way freed from limiting definitions like *fund-raiser, allocator, charity* and *umbrella organization.* Imagine instead a united community process. Not United Way organization with a big *U* and a big *W,* but a community process with a small *u* and a small *w* that enables us to help care for one another.

Imagine a process that is much greater than the sum of its traditional labels and roles: a community process that involves *all* people—that unites whole cities and towns in shaping a common vision of a caring community and in bringing that vision to pass.

Imagine a United Way that widens bridges of community understanding, reinforces social bonds and lifts a community's cooperative and giving spirit to new heights.

Imagine a United Way that sees community needs clearly and can articulate those needs in a way that generates the willing involvement of all the community's resources.

Imagine a United Way that makes services available to all people, that is relevant to their present and future needs, that is pro-active, that does not resist change but embraces it.

Imagine a United Way that works toward representing *all* constituencies in the community, that is polyinfluential, that can gather commitment from every base of citizen support. Imagine an organization whose volunteer leadership extends into every corner of the nation, forging productive partnerships with the widest range of voluntary and political organizations.

Imagine a United Way that, by lifting the flag of community, harmonizes special interests, depolarizes the community and helps build consensus.

A number of years ago I went back to my hometown of Worcester, Massachusetts, for a United Way kick-off. A United Way banner was hung across the street, but gusts of wind kept tearing it down. Then it

occurred to someone to cut holes in the banner. The wind passed through it, and the banner stayed in place.

Like that banner, the more open to change United Way organizations are, and the more open we are to diverse groups of people and the agencies that serve them, the stronger, more resilient—and responsive—we become.

If we can imagine a united way, small *u* small *w,* we can build it. In many communities, the building of this united process has already begun.

United Way *is* becoming that even more open, caring organization. And we're discovering new uses for familiar abilities: our inherent community-building character, our fund-raising know-how, our ability to involve large numbers of people, our ability to communicate need and to allocate resources sensibly.

These abilities are not new. United Ways have been using and refining them for a hundred years. But now we see helping to unify communities as one of our major objectives.

And we are beginning to realize that this community process is what America needs to rebuild itself.

CHAPTER TWO

The Great American Paradox

Since United Way began a century ago, America became the first country in the world to produce what could reasonably be called a mass aristocracy. The kind of prosperity and leisure that had for centuries been the privilege of a tiny layer at the top came to be enjoyed by millions. It was an altogether new phenomenon, and in the greatest multiple migration in history, millions of people from every corner of the globe came to participate in it.

It has been this massive influx of people seeking to better their own lives and raise the quality of life for others that has distinguished American experience.

We have greater resources more widely shared than any nation in history. But, in stark and disturbing contrast to that general picture of prosperity and stability, we have some grim and perplexing problems.

The homeless and hungry have never been so

visible. Nearly two million Americans need food or shelter. Some of the homelessness is temporary, but nearly half the homeless suffer problems of mental instability that could keep them on the streets indefinitely. The causes are complex. As a Pittsburgh social worker said, "Some people are on the street because they drink, others drink because they are on the street."

The homeless themselves are only the tip of the iceberg of poverty. As many as fifty million people may live on or below the poverty level, almost one American in four.

Every eighteen seconds a woman is beaten in America.

Every week forty teenagers give birth to their *third* child. One baby in ten is born to a teenage mother.

There are more than a million runaways in the United States. More than half leave home because of physical neglect. Many have simply been "thrown away" by unstable parents.

According to the National Institute of Mental Health, every ninety seconds a teenager commits suicide.

Many of our older people live lives stunted by fear and loneliness.

Drugs control the minds of staggering numbers of people. One hotline volunteer got a call from a twenty-three-year-old woman who said she had sold her baby for $5,000 to buy cocaine. Crack, or smokable cocaine, is becoming America's latest destructive fad.

The National Institute on Alcohol Abuse places the number of alcoholics in America at almost eighteen million, and the number of children of problem drinkers at twenty-eight million. Alcohol abuse is not only America's No. 1 living-room nightmare, it accounted for an anguishing half of all automobile fatalities in 1985.

This paradox of distress and despair for some amid prosperity for most has been gnawing away at the national conscience for decades.

In the sixties it exploded in intense political activism followed by a disquieting crisis of confidence in American institutions. Veteran political reporter Theodore H. White wrote that what we had once called the Great Society had become "simply a place"—a way of

saying that we had lost our feeling of community. Social psychologist Kenneth Kenniston provided a discouraging wrap-up: "The sixties did not produce a determination to improve society through concerted collective action. On the contrary, most Americans have fallen back on that older American fantasy of the lone cowboy seeking personal fulfillment in an empty desert." We began to speak of the "Me" generation.

But then a different and contrary picture began to emerge. A friend of mine saw a car with two bumper stickers. One said, "Honk if you love narcissism." But next to it was a Red Cross sticker shaped like a drop of blood which said, "I gave the gift of life."

No fewer than eighty-nine million members of the "Me" generation are giving their time and money to support hundreds of thousands of volunteer organizations.

There are people who need help; there are people who want to help. In Albuquerque, the highest percentage of calls taken by the United Way Information and Referral service came from people in need of emergency assistance. The second highest percentage of calls came from people who either wanted to volunteer or who wanted to make donations of clothes, food or money. A Dallas United Way hotline received 77,000 calls for assistance last year. Well over half of them came from people trying to get help for someone other than themselves.

More than 600,000 adults serve as Girl Scout volunteers, and the "Me" generation gives 4,125 gallons of blood a day, *every* day of the year.

The average family in America gives $500 a year to causes they care about. *All* the inmates in a Dade County prison gave up their meals for a day so that $3,000 could be sent to the starving in Ethiopia.

We can begin to see a pattern. Whenever a case of individual distress becomes visible *and* an effective way to help is clear, Americans respond just as willingly in the twentieth century as they did in the nineteenth when there were barns to be raised or fields to be cleared.

The impulse is there. We are not even close to the

bottom of America's well of goodwill. Pollster Daniel Yankelovich reports evidence of an emerging "ethic of commitment." People want to be involved; they would willingly be part of the solution to the problems in their communities if the remedies are clear and *if* they *know what to do*.

And this is exactly what United Ways are learning to do.

We can continue to open up new channels through which people can work together to restore community. We can continue to define community needs more exactly—quantitatively.

We can raise more money—I believe much more money. We can enlist many more volunteers whose potential for increased service we are just beginning to comprehend. There are millions of young people, highly skilled early retirees and healthy older Americans whose energy is still untapped.

We can help mobilize America. And as we do, United Way can give new hope and confidence to the extraordinary network of voluntary organizations that are the key to rebuilding America's dormant sense of community.

CHAPTER THREE

The Meaning of Community

Construction began in 1947 on what would become Levittown, New York—the first suburb. In a matter of a few years, the Levitt Corporation built 17,000 lookalike houses on a 1,200-acre potato field just thirty minutes from Times Square. The building process was so efficient that at one point a new house was completed every fifteen minutes.

Nearly 80,000 people moved into Levitt's houses. Levittown was an instant city; most residents knew no one when they moved there. The people wondered whether it would ever become a community.

In the first nine months of Levittown's existence, fourteen community organizations came into being. By the end of six years, the number had risen to seventy-seven. Nineteen churches were established; so were five elementary schools, two junior high schools and one high school. Local chapters of national organizations like the VFW were formed. A Boy Scout troop was started,

and plans for a YMCA were set in motion. Groups also formed out of special social or practical interests: amateur radio operators started a club, foreign-born wives formed an All-Nations Club, and a Buxom Belle club was created by women wanting to reduce. It was said there was a club for people who did not join clubs. One short decade after Levittown was put—literally—on the map, more than 100 community organizations were in place.

Twenty-five years after the first home was built, 400 of the original home buyers still lived in Levittown. Today this original suburb is in many ways a model *community*.

Community is a sense of belonging without sacrificing individuality. It is a spirit of interdependence converging with a spirit of independence. Community exists when people in a city, town, neighborhood or block care for each other, help each other, believe in each other. A sense of community is a sense that the members of a community are one another's keepers.

Participation in the life of the town is the key. The developer of Columbia, Maryland, James Rouse, earned such a reputation for promoting citizen participation that he was accused, only half in jest, of building "planned mistakes" into his projects so the community would have to learn to work together to fix them.

Where a sense of community exists, frustrations are not as overpowering, a sense of isolation is reduced, stress becomes more bearable. Community is a place, but it is also a connection between hearts. And the community organization is a vital starting point in establishing this connection.

Levittowners, in organizing associations that fit their particular needs, were simply repeating an American experience that has taken place since the earliest colonizations: The continuous forming, dissolving, shaping and reshaping of community organizations has created a dynamic and fertile landscape that in scope and diversity is not equaled anywhere else in the world. United Way is an integral part of this varied terrain of organizations.

We've begun to call these voluntary organizations a sector, comparable in importance to the government sector and the commercial sector. Call this third sector what you will—voluntary, not-for-profit or independent—it is a vast system that includes as many as 7 million organizations, owns one-ninth of all this country's property and employs 4.6 million people. These numbers are estimates. The entities that comprise the sector are always changing.

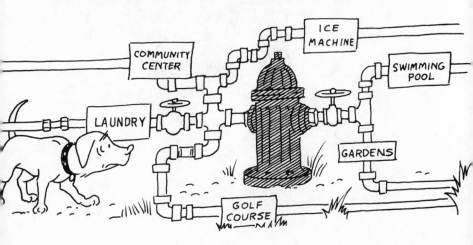

The most visible components of the sector are the nearly 350,000 formally organized voluntary groups that function in every field of human service: from health and welfare to recreation and education, from the extension of human rights to the protection of endangered wildlife, from consumer awareness to the enrichment of culture.

This highly organized subsector has an overall budget of $130 billion. It comprises five percent of America's GNP and exceeds the budgets of all but seven nations. It is a sector that was propelled by 8.4 billion hours of volunteer work last year, conservatively estimated to be worth $110 billion.

Voluntary organizations are instruments of the people. They are created as spontaneous expressions of the concerns of the people. Their activities are sustained by the energies and resources of the people.

Voluntary organizations have no one "role." They accept no limiting definition. They pursue no restricting specialty. But they have certain unique qualities. They have traditionally operated with unusual agility and imagination. Their response to human need is uniquely humane and practical.

But, perhaps most important, voluntary organizations provide the principle channel or mechanism through which literally millions of Americans can "make a difference" by becoming involved in remedying the problems they see about them. Citizens participate not only in decision-making, but increasingly in direct, personal service.

United Way is a central organization in this vast and fluid sector, but by no means the dominant one. And United Way is as complex in structure and texture as the larger sector itself.

CHAPTER FOUR

What United Way is Becoming

The first United Way–type fund-raising organization was a response to a community crisis. Denver—a town that had grown from 5,000 to 100,000 in seven years—could not meet the needs of its residents and its boom-town fortune hunters. Sporadic hat passing was not enough. A group of clergymen tried a new approach (which had worked in Liverpool, England, in 1877)—a combined fund-raising appeal: a single, short-term campaign to raise funds for food, shelter and medical supplies. That's how United Way's original ancestor was born in 1887.

At the same time, predecessors of United Way's allocations arm were being started. As far back as 1873, the influential Cleveland and Bethel Relief Association recommended that there should be a single organization in that city for "investigation and distribution" of charitable funds. But perhaps because of America's familiar ambivalence about freedom and regulation, the first modern Community Chest was not established until forty years later in 1913 in Cleveland. Newton D. Baker, who became Cleveland's mayor that same year, helped create a central volunteer organization that raised funds in a single campaign and distributed them according to a systematic assessment of needs.

Today, there are 2,200 United Way organizations across the country. Every organization is itself autonomous. Although they share many common community objectives, each organization is decidedly different from the others. No two fund-raising campaigns are the same. All allocate money to meet health and human-care needs, yet each has its own way of defining its needs.

Some United Ways have long histories of community service, others are newly formed. Some have come into existence as a result of a single catastrophic event: The Miami Valley flood of 1913 led to the formation of the United Way of the Dayton Area.

One United Way was started recently by a wealthy businessman who was sent to prison for vote buying. He served his time and moved to a United Way–supported halfway house in a county that bordered his own. It was his first contact with United Way. He gave a substantial sum to renovate the halfway house, and a

few months later he started a United Way in his own county, which had never had one before!

There is no such thing as a quintessential United Way. While the United Way of Tri-State, which serves the New York metropolitan area, raised $161 million in 1986, some United Ways raise less than $1,000.

Staff size varies enormously. A few of the largest United Ways have more than fifty paid staff members. But almost 600 United Ways are kept going by a few volunteers and an occasional part-time staff person.

Some United Ways own their buildings. Others make do with a spare room. Many share their facilities with the local Chamber of Commerce or with the agencies they help finance. One United Way is headquartered in a hay barn. And the Quachinta Area United Way in Arkansas works from the back room of the county sheriff's department, the supplies locked in a nearby cell.

A single United Way can serve a very small area or a very large one. By far the most expansive organization is the United Way of Navajo Nation, which serves

165,000 Navajos living on a reservation larger than all New England.

Nor is there a limit to the number of United Ways a state or county can form. The United Way of the Bay Area covers a vast five-county region of California, but there are five United Ways in the single Miami County region of Ohio. There are 107 member United Ways in Ohio, but Rhode Island and Delaware have just one apiece. There may be as many as 300 United Way–type organizations in Minnesota, making it seem like there is one at every crossroads.

Nowhere is the eclectic nature of United Way more apparent than in the variety of programs and services United Way supports. So varied is the list of allocations that United Way of America has a special computer sort

that calls up unclassifiable allocations. At last count, member United Ways supported 333 programs and services that could not be placed in any formal category.

Wherever there is a need there is a United Way allocation. United Ways finance food banks and soup kitchens, neighborhood day care centers and community-wide hotlines. A United Way in Alaska supports a rehabilitation center for Eskimos, and a United Way in West Virginia supports an assistance program for coal-mining families.

A 1986 IRS computer run lists 72,768 tax-exempt organizations that provide health and human-care services. United Way allocations help sustain more than half of them—37,000, by United Way of America's own cautious estimates.

It is not uncommon for a United Way in a small town to support a library or a volunteer fire department, for a large metropolitan United Way to support programs that curb youth gang violence. One town in South Carolina supports two cemeteries, one Catholic and the other Protestant, with equal sums going to each. Dozens of United Ways support counseling programs for widows and widowers; scores support camps for disadvantaged youth; hundreds support women's crisis centers.

Some United Way allocations teams have rigid deadlines for agencies to submit budgets and requests. Others convene and make decisions informally. The number of people involved in the allocations process varies like everything else. The United Way of Suburban Chicago is composed of ninety United Ways with 585 volunteers taking part in the decision-making process.

It is a very touchy thing to allocate donations that come from all sections of a community, particularly if you have never done it before. I once received a letter from a man in a small town in Minnesota who had a lot of questions. He wanted to know when he should make payments to the more than twenty organizations on an allocations list that the previous treasurer left him. He wanted to know if it was all right to support groups such as the Scouts and his community ambulance fund. And he wanted to know if it was all right to keep some money in the bank for emergencies. The amount he had to work with was $2,450.

If there is a characteristic common to all United Ways, it is the sheer number of programs each United Way supports. Even the smallest United Ways make ten or twelve different allocations. A little town near Appleton, Wisconsin, probably holds the record for the breadth of its giving. A total of $5,000 was divided among forty-five agencies. The largest single allocation was $200.

As numerous as the allocations United Ways make are the service partnerships and cooperative arrangements made between United Ways and the agencies on whose behalf money is raised.

At times, United Way of America has helped foster partnerships with other national organizations. Today, United Ways have formed service and fund-raising partnerships with the American Cancer Society (ACS) in more than 100 cities. But ideological differences were so great in the early 1950s that ACS pulled out of the Community Chest umbrella.

Conscientious efforts had been made by my predecessor, Lyman Ford, to meet with ACS leadership to improve relationships and to encourage local linkages. It was important to the Chests that money raised locally be used locally for direct services. Equally important to ACS was that money be allowed to go out of the community to forward research. ACS also resisted line-by-line scrutiny of their budgets by Community Chest boards.

ACS's outstanding chief professional officer for twenty-five years, Lane W. Adams, and I met in the early seventies with a view to finding resolutions to our differences. Lane had been volunteer national treasurer of ACS when it pulled out of the Chest campaigns. Lane had also been an active Community Chest volunteer in Salt Lake. He more than anyone, understood both our organizations' ideologies.

Lane set a precedent by letting me talk to a key ACS committee about United Way and its future directions. It was a ground-breaking effort to overcome historical animosity—and it worked. After several staff-level meetings, I remember going to a flip chart and listing all the nonnegotiables, as well as negotiables, between our two organizations. The ice started to break. We tested the market. In 1977, the first United

Way/ACS agreement in business and industry was struck between the Dallas United Way and ACS in Texas. Lane Adams deserves the plaudits of this nation for his statesmanship and his concern for all who suffer or risk suffering from cancer. The renewed partnership between ACS and United Way is one of the most important chapters in the history of voluntarism. Together we are furthering cancer research and saving lives.

Health and human-service agencies and United Ways depend on one another. Our service agendas are intertwined and inseparable. Millions receive health screenings at work due to cooperative arrangements between employers, United Ways and local chapters of national health agencies. Nearly 150 United Ways offer management assistance to local nonprofits. United Ways work to link skilled employees employed outside the voluntary sector with nonprofit human-service organizations. In St. Louis, fifteen Monsanto Company employees helped agencies refine organizational record-keeping techniques, taught management skills, even held seminars on how to handle job stress and avoid burnout. United Way of Tri-State, in New York, arranged for building engineers at AT&T Long Lines to teach energy conservation techniques to the League School of Brooklyn and other agencies.

United Way executives and agency counterparts are in daily contact. United Ways could not conduct needs assessments without the cooperation of a community's network of agencies. Public awareness campaigns are often joint efforts. Public policy lobbying is almost always a group effort. United Ways help Red

Cross chapters publicize blood shortages. Scout troops carry United Way flags in parades. Girl Scouts in Richmond can earn a United Way merit badge. Salvation Army bands play at United Way kick-offs. United Way publications carry monthly calendars of events sponsored by the YMCA.

Through the Emergency Food and Shelter National Board Program, United Ways worked with agencies to transform $250 million from the federal government into 205 million meals and 47 million nights' lodging. The program is still going on, with United Ways and more than seven thousand agencies working in synchrony.

In many cities, United Way volunteers and staff meet regularly with agency counterparts. Volunteers who serve on a United Way's board often are agency volunteers as well. I take part in meetings that involve the national executives from twenty-seven voluntary health and human-service agencies. We air frustrations and share game plans. Most importantly, we reaffirm what we sometimes forget—that each of our organizations have important, though often independent, functions to perform in communities and that we need each other.

The United Way process has proven exportable. There are over 185 United Ways operating in fifteen countries.

The United Way of Northwest England has been managed almost single-handedly for three decades by a retired draper. The much younger United Way in York is kept going by two high-spirited retirees, one from the British rail system, the other a former city administrator.

The Community Chest in Singapore was started in 1983 by a twenty-four-year-old woman named Bee Wan who had seen the United Way in action as a student at the University of Wisconsin. The president of the Republic of Singapore became its patron-in-chief. It's payroll deduction scheme, called the SHARE Programme (Social Help and Assistance Raised by Employees), generated almost $2.3 million in 1985.

United Ways in Japan can trace their beginnings to General MacArthur. When United States troops occupied Japan, MacArthur instituted a Community Chest to help promote pluralism. In the first campaign, hundreds of Japanese were sent out into the streets with tin cans to collect contributions. They were wildly enthusiastic at first and then crestfallen when they found they couldn't keep the money.

Ballooning requests for technical assistance overseas led United Way of America to establish an international arm in 1974 with its own volunteer board of directors and two full-time staff members. Some of our best overseas consultants are retired United Way executives.

Some United Ways outside the United States begin quietly, others are launched with great fanfare. The launching of a United Way in Baroda, India, lasted ten days. United Way banners were stretched across the Baroda streets and every morning at eight-thirty the local radio station played a United Way song composed for the occasion. The main kick-off drew 400,000.

The community process United Way has pioneered is becoming international, and what we do in the next hundred years with what we have learned will have worldwide consequences.

CHAPTER FIVE

Space-Age Fund-Raising

United Way campaigns now raise more than $2.5 billion a year nationwide. Along the way, they show United Way volunteers and staff at their most creative.

Campaigns are life-giving phenomena: full of heart, bursting with spirit. Raising money by selling off portions of the world's largest submarine sandwich, which happened in Philadelphia, or letting loose 1.5 million balloons, which happened in Cleveland, says something refreshing about the spirit of our movement.

Some campaigns have necessarily evolved into meticulously planned undertakings and lost the innocence of a spontaneous pass-the-hat solicitation. But no matter how businesslike or tactical a campaign is, there is something exciting and lyrical about a community-wide effort to raise money for a worthy cause.

Organized charitable fund-raising is a relatively new phenomenon. Its beginnings were British. The inaugural attempt at a cooperative charitable fund-raising effort was vetoed flatly by most of London's 400 social agencies in 1869. Eight years later the first successful plan for central financing was carried out by the Central Relief Society in Liverpool. The campaign proved conclusively that community agencies could raise more money together than separately. The principle still holds true.

Decades later came another breakthrough: the realization that short campaigns raised more money than protracted ones. In 1926, Cleveland showed the way by conducting a heavily publicized short-term campaign in the fall, beginning around Labor Day and ending on Thanksgiving.

Some of the most impressive United Way efforts in recent years have compressed the public campaign into very short periods of time. So fervor has no chance to exhale. Before the public campaign, pre-campaigning through brisk pacesetter programs and education programs are used to whip up enthusiasm throughout the

community. United Way of America had its most successful in-house campaign to date in 1985. The kick-off was at nine-thirty in the morning, employees were solicited during the next two hours, and we had our victory the next afternoon at four. The education process was a month long, but the drive itself took less than thirty-two hours.

The mechanism for payroll deductions was put into place in 1943. That was the great watershed that quickly democratized giving. Before payroll deduction most of the money raised in campaigns came from the wealthy. Solicitations were limited to a small pool of large givers. Today, nearly half the money raised for charities comes from people who earn less than $30,000. Payroll deduction might have ushered in the tired joke about giving at the office, but it also turned the average worker into a philanthropist.

A few years ago, Bill Shannon, then U.S. Ambassador to Ireland, arranged for me to talk with a group of businessmen in Dublin. I started my presentation about

the value of the United Way system and how it can transform communities. A gruff Irishman stood up and asked why he should give. Why should he duplicate his government's welfare efforts? Wasn't the government responsible?

While I was fumbling around for an answer, another Irish businessman stood up. He had worked on the line in an American factory that ran a United Way campaign. "Imagine", he said, "*I* was asked to give! I was an average worker and I become a philanthropist! I felt great pride. For me giving was a great privilege."

That Irishman would not have endorsed United Way if he had been forced to give. Many United Ways have written and unwritten codes discouraging coercion. For example, the United Way of King County,

Seattle, issued a public statement on the issue. It reads in part: "United Way of King County discourages the practice of seeking 100-percent participation in the organization. This process encourages token giving or, even worse, results in pressure to give. It is important to remember, not everyone can or will contribute." Giving that comes from hearts that care and minds that understand is the most valid kind.

United Ways and other voluntary organizations lobbied hard for a tax code that gives all taxpayers, whether they itemize or not, the same right to deduct charitable gifts. The impact of the 1986 Tax Reform Act could very well lead to a drop in contributions, particularly from larger givers. A study by Harvard's Lawrence Lindsey projects losses of up to $11 billion because of these changes. Yet I'm confident that generous giving will continue. The impetus to contribute will become a matter for the individual's conscience rather than his or her accountant. While I was in Hong Kong in August 1986, three Hong Kong business leaders wrote checks for $250,000 to support United Way's international program. When I asked one of them why he gave so much, he said that his country had been very good to him. The historically low tax rate in Hong Kong had allowed him and his father to further their business. He was grateful for the opportunity to help others.

Single workplace campaigns continue to provide United Ways with the majority of their funds. But they have never been the only means of raising money, and there are many United Ways in small cities that do not use payroll deductions at all.

Some of the supplementary avenues for raising money are strictly practical; others are wildly ingenious. There are United Ways in Wisconsin that have been raising money for years from dairy farmers who figure their United Way contributions as a percentage of the total gallons of milk they sell to their area dairy cooperative. For years the United Way campaign in Decatur, Illinois, built a big bin for corn in the middle of town. The corn was sold and the proceeds given to United Way. Ocala, Florida, is horse country. Breeders pledge stud fees—some as high as $50,000—to United Way. Montana cattle and sheep farmers pledge an amount for each

head of livestock they raise. And United Way fund-raisers in cities with motels and hotels routinely ask owners to give so much per room as a corporate contribution. In New Orleans, campaigners fly to off-shore oil rigs in helicopters and conduct group solicitations.

The key is to identify markets where people are and to create opportunities. In Miami Beach there are a lot of people who live somewhere else and spend a few weeks in Miami. When I was the executive of Dade County's United Way, a typical response to a solicitation call was, "Look, I'm from somewhere else. I give to the United Way in my hometown. I'm only here for a couple of months."

We made a list of all the reasons people gave for not giving and created an organization called the "Golden Wagon." To be a member, you had to be from another community, you had to be giving to your United Way in that community and you had to reside in Miami for only part of the year. We took every negative reason and made it a positive condition of membership. Jim Knight, the chairman of Knight-Ridder newspapers, took the lead and made the Golden Wagon idea come alive. He personally hosted and paid for a reception and name band, and everyone had a ball. We asked for a minimum of $1,000. One woman, who had given us $25 before, gave $5,000. We made $250,000 the first year.

United Way democratized giving, but somewhere along the way we passed over those with the means to give more. It wasn't until 1984 that Dr. Thomas Frist, chairman of Hospital Corporation of America, started a program in Nashville for major givers.

Big givers and small givers alike need to feel that their contribution matters. Dr. Frist's objective was for people of high net worth to give enough to cover all the overhead costs of that United Way, so that 100 percent of employee contributions would go directly to services. Those who contributed $10,000 or more were inducted into the Alexis de Tocqueville Society. Now there are similar programs in thirty-five cities. In just two years, the number of people giving $10,000 or more grew from 360 to 1359. And now nearly twenty individuals each give $100,000 or more a year.

That's just one example of how necessity is forcing us to change our familiar fund-raising practices. We must begin to break rules we made ourselves.

CHAPTER SIX

The X Factor

The corporate landscape is changing.

When businesses are broken down according to size, the result is a very squat pyramid, and it is getting squatter. There are roughly 3 million corporations in America. Only 800 have sales of $1 billion or more, and only around 15,000 have sales of between $25 million and $1 billion. All the rest are small- and medium-sized companies with relatively few employees. And businesses are decentralizing and downsizing. The result: more doors to knock on and fewer people behind each door.

United Ways have concentrated on the fraction of companies at the upper part of the pyramid—organizations with the highest concentration of employees. Some United Ways have tried to reach every business in their community, but they tend to find their volunteers being spread too thin. When I came to Miami, there was a campaign structure designed to cover 23,000 businesses, but we simply lacked the manpower to campaign so broadly. Instead, we focused on just

2,000 firms. The results were impressive. But I'm convinced that there are enough volunteer resources in Miami to reach every one of those 23,000 businesses.

Getting the word out to businesses with 500, 100, 50, 20, or fewer employees will require rethinking our staffing, our recruiting efforts and our management methods. We have to keep our fund-raising cost-effective. We still have to run efficient campaigns. We always have to be hard as nails on efficiency. But we will need to spend more money to raise new dollars. At the same time, United Way direct services must not suffer. Training programs, community problem-solving initiatives, needs assessments, employee assistance programs and other services deserve to be financed at even higher levels than before and must become even more of an organizational focus. Raising new money and delivering more direct services mean that something has to give. Administration and fund-raising costs will temporarily go up.

The biggest problem of the older cities in the Midwest and Northeast is, paradoxically, their history of effectiveness. They are the highest per-capita-giving cities in the United States. Now they are facing a dilemma. The old industries are getting smaller as the high-per-capita-giving firms cut employment to survive.

These United Ways are recognizing that they cannot raise money the way they used to. They are developing new methods designed for these new, tougher, higher-cost fund-raising markets. They are accepting the fact that they must be willing to spend more for new, but harder-to-get dollars. Even if the cost for those last, hardest-to-get dollars is 20–25 percent, their low average fund-raising cost will not be significantly increased. So they are analyzing their opportunities market by market and determining what each will cost. They are rethinking how to make the best use of volunteer time and expertise to reach these new resources.

The more than $2 billion that United Ways raise is about three percent of all charitable gifts. Yet United Way allocations provided the core support for agencies with annual budgets totaling more than $20 billion. Our dollars create a multiplier effect—a yeastlike quality that keeps the direct human service portion of the voluntary sector financially stable.

In today's competitive world, United Way still offers the most cost-efficient way to generate resources to build a community pool of money, unlinked to any specific cause, that can be allocated according to community needs as they arise. A package of "asks" is put together for the community, not just a series of individual "asks."

There seems to be an X factor of legitimacy that comes when your cause is the betterment of the community. For whatever reason, corporations and individuals do far more for a single community-wide campaign than for individual causes.

United Ways generated $550 million new dollars in the past three years—the best net real campaign

growth in our history. We are raising money more effectively than ever. We are segmenting our markets. We are constantly refining an already well-oiled process. But we can't take our access and campaign privileges at the workplace for granted.

We are strong, but we aren't invulnerable. In the face of competition and change, United Way has to re-earn employer and community respect every year by becoming *more* responsive to human needs.

Valuable as money is, there is a more essential, if less tangible, value of the single community-wide campaign. The product of campaigns is a dollars-and-cents figure. But the by-product—the greater product—is a breaking down of barriers that cause alienation, ambivalence and disunity.

A special United Way fund-raising event in New York gave 5,000 Asians a chance to hear Hong Kong's most popular contemporary singer. In the process, a new segment of New York society was introduced to United Way. Toronto's United Way/Centraid arranged a concert featuring India's most popular singer. Editorials in Toronto newspapers said the event was one of the best things to happen to that city in years.

If I were asked to list the values of a single community campaign for health and human-care services, I would certainly cite low-cost fund-raising and the efficient involvement of volunteers to raise a maximum amount of money—in short, more bang for the charitable buck and the wise use of people's precious time and energy. But there is a far greater value that goes beyond efficiency and effectiveness, as important

as they are. The United Way campaign gives people a chance to understand the needs of their fellow citizens and, most importantly, a chance to unite the community.

Black, Hispanic, Asian, European, white collar, blue collar, suburban, urban, Catholic, Protestant, Moslem, Jew, young, old, immigrant—United Way campaigns unify a community. They inspire concern. They build bridges. They create goodwill. They reveal the human spirit at its very best.

CHAPTER SEVEN

Facts About The Future

What do we know about America? We know there are 226.5 million people living here. We know that they have grouped themselves into 85 million households. We know that 27 percent of these households are single or unrelated people living together. We know too that there are 6.6 million single parents raising nearly 15 million children—two-thirds more than ten years ago.

We know who earns how much. We know that nearly 40 million people live in what we have officially defined as poverty.

We know that immigration is accelerating. Twenty years ago, more than half of all immigrants came from Europe and Canada. Today, most are Mexicans, Chinese, Vietnamese, Koreans, Indians, Filipinos, Dominicans and Jamaicans.

We know that the minority population in this nation has grown 56 percent in the last twelve years.

We know that after a half century of centralization, there is a gathering tendency toward decentralization.

The era of automatic increases in federal spending for human services is almost certainly over. Gramm-Rudman-Hollings is the New Deal of the 1980s.

But most of all we know that change is not something that is *going* to happen—change *is* happening!

More than 12.000 new businesses are launched each week, nearly one-third by women.

Companies are changing their management structures. Middle managers are becoming an endangered species.

Whole job categories are disappearing. There were 17,000 photoengravers and stereographic workers in 1972. By 1982 there were only 3,200.

Professional routines are changing. Lawyers can advertise. Chain stores like K-Mart are hiring dentists. Their patients shop while they wait until they're summoned by borrowed beepers.

Getting cancer once meant *dying* from cancer. Today, a reunion of Americans who have survived cancer would fill a city the size of Los Angeles.

Twenty-five years ago there were no shopping

malls. Today they are everywhere. Rand McNally puts the large ones on its maps, right alongside cities and towns. In fact, the mall has become the closest example of community many people experience: Mall-town's streets are clean; its atmosphere exudes prosperity, neighborliness and vitality.

Our perception of the whole universe is changing. A university astronomy professor confided that as a result of the Voyager missions and other satellite data, a full half of what he taught five years ago was already out of date.

Needs themselves come, go and come again. Many United Ways are having to provide the basics of food and shelter in the wake of great layoffs in heavy industry. The number of people requesting emergency food and lodging in Pittsburgh has more than tripled in the last two years. In fact, United Ways have doubled the amount of money allocated to support emergency-related programs between 1980 and 1985. A half century after the Great Depression, United Ways have suddenly found themselves back in the soup kitchen business.

John W. Gardner, former Secretary to HEW, and a good friend to voluntarism, has reminded us that in the past quarter century we began to work systematically and analytically to resolve human problems and conflicts. In the mid-seventies, United Ways and the voluntary sector began to look at human problems strategically, planning agendas that break out of the twelve-month pattern of raising money, allocating money and raising money again.

United Way's first Strategic Planning program was launched by United Way of America in 1976, under the leadership of John W. Hanley, then chairman of the board and president of Monsanto Company. The program aimed to define the most pressing issues then facing the United Way movement. A survey of United Ways produced more than 200 responses and identified about 120 issues. These worked their way into the plans and programs of United Ways all across the country.

Environmental scanning is an even newer process to United Ways. It goes beyond organizational planning to ask: Where is the world coming from? How does the external environment, the extra-organizational environment, affect what we are doing?

The importance of scanning was illustrated by the life insurance industry when it perceived a mysterious inexplicable market decline. From the inside-out perspective of the industry, it didn't make sense. The economy was growing. The population was growing. The baby boom was just entering the labor market, adding millions of potential new customers. Yet per-capita sales of life insurance were lagging this growth. Research revealed a fundamental social change—the emergence of the wife as a permanent second earner in many families. The life insurance needs of the family with one income are much greater than those of the family protected by two.

Much of life is predictable. But action must coincide with predictions. There are 6.6 million single-parent households in America. What does that mean to an organization like United Way? Are we focusing on child care? What are the real needs in this area?

Peter Drucker has made the point that the lead times of demographic events are known. Every person

who will be in the American labor force by the year 2000 has already been born. It is up to social organizations to make a healthy use of this piece of demographics.

In the last few years, significant environmental scan studies have been conducted by United Way of America and other national agencies, including Boys' Clubs of America, Girl Scouts of the U.S.A., Easter Seals, Catholic Charities/USA, Volunteers of America, the American Red Cross and the Council of Jewish Federations, Inc.

Among United Ways, the number engaging in strategic planning has more than doubled since 1980—from slightly more than 200 to almost 500. Five years ago, fewer than ten United Ways raising $100,000 or less had strategic planning programs. Today, more than 200 of the smallest United Ways have them. A group of volunteers in Ocala, Florida, created an annual report that highlighted what they thought their United Way could accomplish in the year 2000.

No matter how sophisticated a system an organization develops for predicting long-term results, decisions about service delivery must be built on a solid foundation of fact. We cannot act on hunch or conjecture or on what we used to call windshield surveys of distressed communities. We need to know who *exactly* is in what kind of trouble, which entities and therapies are most likely to succeed.

Through Project Flagship, United Ways are establishing uniform, comprehensive data bases that profile both supporters and users of human service programs. Flagship links United Way of America and local United Ways to a computerized database on more than 2000 human-service providers, whose combined annual budgets exceed $2 billion, and we are just beginning.

The payoff has been almost immediate. Due to the technology of Flagship, Chattanooga now has its first client information system on child sexual abuse. Prevention efforts can be focused where we know they are most needed.

Social-service dollars are difficult to track because they come from so many sources. As Flagship's database grows, a much clearer picture of where money

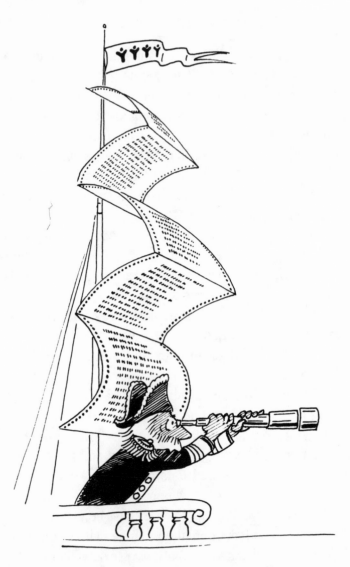

comes from and where it goes is taking shape. Cleveland now knows that for every United Way dollar that is put toward services to the elderly, various government sources put in $2.50. San Francisco knows that for every dollar its United Way puts toward services to the elderly, various government sources put in $13.

Flagship data is helping United Ways document their support of various community groups. For example, of the 200 agencies that Detroit's United Way supported in 1981, fifty-two served Hispanics through eighty-two programs.

And in April of 1985, United Way of America and Mutual of America established a nationwide telecommunications network of not-for-profits. Called the Human Care Network, it makes human-service databases immediately accessible to users. Information can be sent back and forth to any of the hundreds of users. Through the network, electronic mass mailings have recently gone out that instantly informed United Ways about tax legislation and other issues of organizational importance.

But it isn't enough to look ahead and know the facts. As new circumstances bring new problems, we have to invent new ways to deal with them. As a nation, we have done a lot of social inventing and adapting. The inventive spirit has been constant. Small contrivances have had huge consequences. We tremble when we hear about inventions that displace people. But the crucial inventions are of an opposite order, those that *involve* more people more fully in the world's work.

The use of carts on wheels in grocery stores revolutionized retailing by democratizing it. Millions of shoppers became involved in selecting and fetching merchandise. There are many other such inventions: fire extinguishers, vending machines, typewriters, home freezers and hundreds more. Payroll deduction was another such invention. United Way itself was another.

In the 1940s, through the foresight of my predecessor Ralph Blanchard, the Retirement Association was born. Envisioned to be a caretaking organization for the caretakers, it began with an interest-free loan of $25,000. Then in 1945, a group of concerned businessmen, none of whom had any insurance background, formed Mutual of America. Before that time, people could work their whole lives for a nonprofit social-service organization and have little to retire on. Today, Mutual of America serves the entire nonprofit sector. Under the dynamic leadership of William J. Flynn, Mutual of America has grown to become one of the fifty largest insurance providers in the country.

United Ways are constantly inventing ingenious new ways to do business. United Ways in twelve small Arkansas communities could not afford to hire a full- or even part-time professional, so they developed Project Circuit Rider. One United Way professional was shared between twelve United Ways. She logged more than 30,000 miles in her car, spending six weeks at each participating United Way, helping them in every aspect of their work, from fund-raising to allocations.

In 1983 United Way of America helped organize a separate tax-exempt organization called Gifts in Kind to broker gifts of merchandise from businesses to non-profit organizations—whether funded by United Ways or not. The 3M company has donated more than 6000 copiers. Digital Equipment Corporation gave 2500 top-of-the-line printers. Electrolux Corporation has donated

60,000 vacuum cleaners. Most gifts go to small neigh-borhood agencies. Covenant House, a beacon of hope to runaways and street kids in New York, received twelve vacuum cleaners. More than $70 million worth of in-kind donations have been distributed to 25,000 nonprofit organizations. The fear that these donations would reduce cash contributions proved unfounded.

We are *gaining* new confidence in our ability to find new ways to build community in our next hundred years. We're also discovering and developing better ways of management. We are getting better at doing good.

CHAPTER EIGHT

Getting Better At Doing Good

Shared values of community service are at the heart of United Way's organizational culture.

United Way is a sprawling network. There are 2,200 local autonomous units, but no powerful headquarters from which edicts are passed down. Yet there is a sense of unity. United Ways are bound together by a common mission. They have common problems and opportunities. They share certain organizational standards. They agree on certain service strategies; almost all of them display a common logo and subscribe to common goals. Why? How?

Experts in corporate culture will tell you that the way to transform an organization is to articulate a mission, then mobilize commitment around that mission. We were told this by consultants at Peat Marwick & Mitchell just before I became the chief professional officer in the late sixties. At that time, United Way had no name in common and no common mission statement.

To begin to build unity and shared purpose among the volunteers and professionals, United Way needed a

locus for communicating an organizational philosophy, and a training center where philosophy and real life could meet.

Until that time the national association had a small staff that struggled to fill requests for products and information. Membership support was inadequate; we did a good for smaller communities but not for the larger ones.

The first step to shaping a more effective United Way *system* was to reshape the national organization. New leadership was recruited—both volunteer and professional. The board, chaired by the amazing Bayard Ewing, adopted a new name, United Way of America, to reflect not a fund but a process. Community Chests, Good Neighbor Funds, United Funds and Community Funds were asked to subscribe to the name "United Way." Saul Bass, who developed logos for AT&T, United Airlines and Quaker Oats developed a logo for us. When it was first unveiled, some people said,

"Aramony, it looks like a football helmet!" Today, millions know that the helping hand and arching rainbow of hope stand for caring . . . the United Way.

Then United Way formed a partnership with the National Football League. Today, during football season, eighty million people hear about United Way every week through the largest and longest-running public service campaign in history. "Thanks to you it works for all of us . . . the United Way" is a household slogan. The whole nation owes a debt of gratitude to commissioner Pete Rozelle and the NFL for airing these public-service messages—worth $500 million in advertising time—free of charge. For more than half a generation, NFL players have been telling America their own stories of how United Way and its network of services have made a difference in their lives. In doing so they have served as a positive role model for millions.

United Way was gaining an identity. A statement of mission was adopted: "To increase the organized capacity of people to care for one another." Jim Burke,

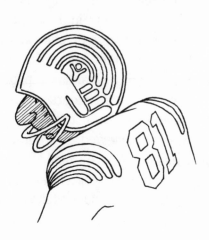

chairman and chief executive officer of Johnson and Johnson, and chairman of our Strategic Planning Committee, told me at the time that this was the best mission statement he had ever seen. Then again, a staff member whose opinion I respected told me you could drive a truck through it. He was right. It puts no arbitrary limit on what United Way can do.

That's the strength of it. The mission statement doesn't talk about fund-raising. It doesn't talk about community planning. It doesn't talk about allocation. It talks about increasing the organized capacity—the community's capacity—of people to care for one another in whatever ways citizens, working together, can devise. The United Way twelve-word statement of mission is a vision of what we *can become* and are becoming!

Over the years this statement of mission has become accepted by the United Way movement as a common overreaching ambition. Today it is the rock on which whatever we do is based. Every innovation begins with it.

A set of strategies for bringing this mission to life has been set. They were born in the trenches of United Way service, the fruit of a two-year exchange of ideas among United Way volunteer and professional leaders.

The process began with an issue paper written by Dr. Lisle Carter—former undersecretary of HEW, United Way volunteer and consultant to United Way of America. Dr. Carter reviewed environmental-trend information and asked: Where should United Way go? Should it continue to do what it knows best—raise money and allocate it? Or should it take our organization to a higher level of service?

The paper was first circulated to United Way leaders—professional and volunteer.

The issues became the topic of United Way of America's Chief Volunteer Officer's Forum in early 1984 and of its Volunteer Leaders Conference in May 1984. Two thousand United Way volunteers attended the Volunteer Leaders Conference. *The* major decision-making body of United Way—its key volunteers—began to reinvent United Way.

Shortly after that, I took the first cut at a paper designed to give life to the mission statement. It laid out five core program activities central to our mission. I called the paper "Rethinking Tomorrow and Beyond." It emphasized the value of the single community-wide campaign for health and human services. But it went beyond that. It urged greater donor choice and more flexible funding. It stressed the need for year-round workplace education about United Way. It urged more involvement of people and agencies. In particular, it focused less on United Way the low-cost community-wide fund-raiser than on United Way the catalyst for solving community problems.

After much review and input by United Way professionals, I presented this draft to the Strategic Planning Committee of United Way of America's Board of Governors. If these strategies were going to work, these volunteer leaders would have to buy in.

They didn't. They challenged the paper; they questioned its relevance. Now I know why. The paper gave no philosophical or historical context for what was being proposed. It presumed a detailed knowledge of our history.

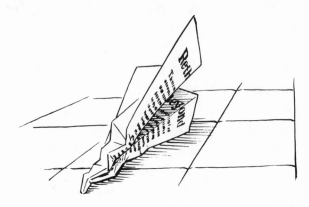

Once an historical overview was added to the document, it was clear that the five core strategies were a logical—almost inevitable—extension of what United Way had been doing for almost a century. Suddenly these issues were discussable. People began to see in them a new course for United Way.

I presented the five revised core strategies to our National Professional Advisory Committee. They helped refine and reshape the five strategies and endorsed them unanimously.

In the spring of 1985, United Way of America's Board of Governors adopted the five core strategies—community problem solving, inclusiveness, the single community-wide campaign, fund distribution and year-round communication—as the means to achieve its mission.

You can't talk about United Way's organizational culture anymore without talking about its five core strategies of service. They have become the *values* that define more precisely our organizational culture.

1. *Community problem solving* recognizes the value of helping people who are hurting.
2. *Inclusiveness* is the right of *all* people to be part of the community.
3. *The single community-wide campaign* gives people an essential chance to reach out to each other and upholds the cherished democratic value of impartial participation.
4. *Fund distribution* affirms the widely shared value of stewardship in society, making sure that the most urgent needs are being met—and that new needs are being anticipated.
5. *Year-round communication* acknowledges that effective giving comes from an understanding heart and a well informed head.

These five strategies—these five values—which flow from the United Way mission, give cohesion to the movement, and guide every aspect of United Way management.

CHAPTER NINE

The Boundless Resource

Despite their low public profile, the number of Americans who volunteer increases with every new poll. Most recently (1985) Gallup put the figure at 89 million Americans who work "in some way to help others for no monetary pay."

A quick flip through recent editions of Volunteer's publication *Voluntary Action Leadership* showed volunteers saving deer by planting bitterbush for forage in Boise National Forest, volunteers working to involve elderly members of the Hispanic community in new programs and "volunteer scribes" assisting those too old or too young to write letters. There was a story about volunteers who made an accurate count of America's spotted owl population. An orthopedic-shoe specialist volunteered his time to drive across the border to Mexico to fit children with braces, special shoes and artificial limbs, and a doctor operated a tattoo-removal program that offered youngsters who could not otherwise afford it the opportunity to have unflattering tattoos surgically removed.

United Way of America's *Community* magazine recently carried stories of United Way volunteers who organized mammoth special events like the "Wall Street Run" in New York that involved seventy-one companies. Volunteers from the Florida Building and Construction Trades Council, AFL-CIO, renovated a twenty-acre Boys Club in Mobile, Alabama; volunteers in Middletown, Ohio, packed 39,115 brown bag lunches to feed hungry children.

For the person who wants to devote the time, there are thousands of options for service.

In 1959, in the most extensive study of life and death ever undertaken, the American Cancer Society enrolled and trained 68,000 volunteers to reach a million Americans. The study unmistakably linked smoking to cancer and pointed the way to preventing nearly a third of cancer deaths. In the fall of 1982, the ACS launched a second study with 1.2 million subjects, this time involving 100,000 volunteers. Without volunteers, the study would have cost more than $100 million, but it is unlikely that it would have been undertaken at all.

Money pressure—the pressure to raise money and the pressure to spend it to get things done—is going to be permanent. If the voluntary sector is going to develop, and if United Way is going to continue to be a leader in that development, it will happen not because we find new resources of money but because we muster our imagination to find new ways to involve volunteers.

A volunteer power base exists that can carry United Way to untold accomplishments of which few of us can conceive. The men and women who, in their commercial capacities, produce a GNP of more than $3 trillion a year make up our power base. This country's youth, the most literate generation America has ever produced, are not only part of our power base for today but our leaders of tomorrow.

In 1985, the Salvation Army organized an international youth conference that drew 5,000 teenagers. And in 1987, United Way of America is sponsoring a youth leaders conference as part of our Centennial Volunteer Leaders Conference. High-schoolers will get a chance to help shape United Way's future. Thousands of Memphis, Tennessee's grade-school children took part in a

United Way program called "A Dime's Worth of Difference." Each child was encouraged to give something, or do something, to help United Way community efforts.

More women than ever are serving as volunteers. The 1982 Gallup survey on voluntarism discovered that women who work are more likely to volunteer than women who do not. The millions of women who are gaining confidence by entering the job market, and who are staying employed much longer, make up a growing part of our volunteer base.

If the community efforts of this volunteer base can be better focused, organized and challenged, there is almost no limit to what can be accomplished.

The Census Bureau has counted 50 million people at or over the age of fifty-five in America. Many have considerable leisure time—not idle time, but time to devote to activities outside of earning a living. Their knowledge, their experience and their talents can be of inestimable worth.

A single retiree involvement program in Arkansas successfully completed forty projects in a year-and-a-half. A group of retired doctors developed plans for a countrywide ambulance service. A group of retired engineers planned a new drainage system after severe floods in the state. Some volunteers with financial backgrounds drew up plans for a joint investment program for twenty city and two county governments.

One of the most successful programs for the homeless and hungry is called Senior Gleaners. Funded by United Way, the all-volunteer organization is dedicated to reducing hunger by gleaning fields and orchards for fruits and vegetables and by salvaging food from retail and wholesale outlets, which would otherwise go to waste. Members must be at least fifty years old, retired and willing to work. As of March 1985 there were 2,300 members, each paying $3 a month to belong. The Senior Gleaners' philosophy is to work with the farmer, not against him. One farmer called to report he had eighty bins of pears on his hands. They were part of a late harvest and would yield only $30 a bin, about the cost of picking. Instead of letting the pears rot on the trees, the farmer called Senior Gleaners. They picked the pears and gave them back to the farmer who, in turn, made a monetary donation to a local food bank. In 1984 alone, Senior Gleaners salvaged close to 8 million pounds of food.

In the book *Habits of the Heart,* a group of social philosophers crisscrossed the United States to find out

where middle American priorities lay. The authors gave the following summation:

> Practically all the people we talked to would agree
> . . .that two of the most basic components of a
> good life are success in one's work and the joy of
> serving one's community. And they would also
> tend to agree that the two are so closely inter-
> twined that a person cannot usually have the one
> without the other.

Yet many people simply don't know where and how they can help. They don't know which organizations need volunteers, when and for how long. We're building systems for filling professional positions with the right people, but we are much farther away from an effective system of volunteer recruiting and placement.

Voluntary opportunities aren't visible enough. Often they're not designed to people's schedules; they are offered at the wrong time or the wrong place. Ours is an era of video rental parlors that never close, all-night Laundromats and convenience stores around every corner. Volunteering can be made much more convenient without becoming less effective.

We know beyond a doubt that volunteering—even in small amounts—results in increased levels of charitable giving. In 1985, the Rockefeller Brothers Fund commissioned Yankelovich, Skelly & White to find out about American giving habits. The average charitable gift of those who did not volunteer was $510. The average gift of those who did volunteer was $850. Volunteers give two-thirds more than nonvolunteers.

How can we make our volunteer opportunities more accessible? One way we've only begun to tap is to link them to America's workplaces. There continues to be no better place for keeping people informed about how United Way works and what United Way and the agencies it works with are capable of accomplishing in a community.

CHAPTER TEN

Company As Community

Making a company a community may be the single biggest management challenge to American business. Large companies have employee bases the size of major cities. Corporations have had to provide many of the same services a responsible community might deliver.

The figures in education are particularly astounding. It has been estimated that 6.3 million employees participate each year in corporate-sponsored educational activities. The American Society for Training and Development estimates that employers in the United States now spend between $30 and $40 billion on education and training for the workforce each year—an amount equal to the total of public spending for colleges and universities.

Before the divestiture, AT&T spent $6 million a year for training in basic mathematics and writing, with a continuous enrollment of 14,000. 10 percent of Polaroid's more than 13,000 employees go to college at the company's expense.

Forbes noted that about sixty big firms now shoulder up to $2000 of the costs for employees who wish to adopt children. Corporate child-care is as old as the Civil War, when munitions manufacturers set up day nurseries for the mothers they employed.

According to the Conference Board's Work and Family Information Center, about 1,800 of more than 6 million U.S. companies provide some form of child-care assistance. Aid ranges from child-care per diems of a few dollars to the vouchers that Polaroid Corporation offers, which cover up to 80 percent of the cost of care at a community child-care center.

Organized labor encourages community service by union employees. The AFL-CIO Department of Community Services reports that 259,363 union members were helped in 1985 through drug and alcohol abuse counseling, personal financial planning, suicide prevention, emergency food and shelter and more.

Value systems inside companies build community. J. C. Penney sustains a feeling of togetherness by upholding the high moral standards on which the company was founded. The first store opened by James Cash Penney was called The Golden Rule. If you work for Penney, you are known as an associate. You are left with no doubt that you have a hand in Penney successes. You learn the J. C. Penney code of ethics by heart.

Johnson & Johnson not only credits its corporate credo for nurturing a sense of community, it credits it with guiding the company through the Tylenol catastrophe. The credo does not talk about profits and losses, but about product quality, safety and customer satisfaction. The corporate response to the first tampering episode was guided by those principles. It led to new packaging standards, and Tylenol quickly regained public confidence.

One of the best ways to strengthen a company's *inside* community is to strengthen the *outside* community where employees and their families live. I'm convinced there is a strong correlation between the presence of United Way inside a company and the social awareness of those who are part of that company.

United Way is only beginning to sense its value to employees and employers *inside* the corporate community. We are only beginning to employ the strategy of inclusiveness that links the United Way operations more completely and intelligently to where givers work and live.

In market after market, United Ways have been living with organizational boundaries based on old-fashioned city, county and state borders. These borders were drawn up in the early days when we traveled by horse and buggy. There were no turnpikes or expressways.

People should know that their United Way contributions or volunteer service helps in the community where they raise their kids and cut their grass. At the same time, money has to follow need. If money raised in one suburb could be better used in another, we should be able to push it there.

I can remember when United Way had a merger mania. We wanted to combine into one big happy family.

It didn't work. Naturally, no United Way wanted to lose its identity. Givers didn't want to support an organization that they couldn't see working. But still our organizational lines weren't corresponding to our constituencies of givers and those in need.

United Ways are becoming wiser. They're drawing new boundaries that create fund-raising partnerships based on natural markets, typically the range of the local television station. The boundaries of these partnerships are not rigid and often cannot be drawn on any map. They are designed to *retain local ownership*. United Way's roots lie in local participation—involvement by citizens in every suburb or city neighborhood. There have been some outstanding examples of how well fund-raising according to work/live patterns can work.

The New York market is a cooperative phenomenon. There are thirty-eight United Ways in New York City, Long Island, New Jersey and southwest Connecticut—all raising money together as one market, with agreed-upon formulas for the money's division. That partnership didn't come easily, there was some fierce resistance. But with fund-raising results running 5 to 10 percent higher every year for the past eight years, its critics are becoming an endangered species.

Philadelphia's areawide partnership has nine partners. In 1980–81 these United Ways separately were showing growth of 3.9 percent. The collective growth in the past four years has been 9.7 percent.

The Boston area is a major success story. It is in its fourth year of an areawide arrangement that includes sixty-five companies (employing 325,000) and twenty-one partner United Ways stretching from Manchester,

New Hampshire to Rhode Island and from Cape Cod to Worcester, Massachusetts. Money—$80 million in 1986—is being distributed by a formula based not just on where employees work but where they live. Increases among partner United Ways have been running five to ten percentage points higher than pre-areawide increases.

As United Ways become better at organizing themselves around not only where people work and are solicited, but also where they live and are apt to volunteer, employees will give more and do more. Whether the money stays in the neighborhood where a person lives or is distributed many miles away, people need to *see* their contributions making a difference.

CHAPTER ELEVEN

United Way At Work

As we learn to help corporations build community, we are changing—radically—the way we do business inside companies.

United Ways are adapting to the wrenching changes at the workplace—the rise of the hands-on employee, the employee who demands to be involved in more ways than checking off a box on a pledge card. United Ways are changing in response to environmental upheavals that left employees feeling closer to their companies, but often alienated from the community as a whole.

We're moving to strategies of *year-round* presence and *year-round* education. Our studies of the workplace tell us that once nongivers know how our system works—including the allocations process—70 percent of these nongivers become givers. And when givers *better* understand the process, they give even more.

A revolutionary United Way program was started at the GM plant in Flint, Michigan, in the late seventies.

I was invited to pull employees off the GM line and talk to them about it. They were enthusiastic; they liked the United Way employee involvement program; they understood the United Way process. The workers who did volunteer work were glad to be recognized for it and to find that other employees felt the same.

The United Way presence at the workplace—United Way at Work—offers everyone a chance to put an oar in the water. These programs are not disguised fund-raising ventures. They meet real needs. They require the endorsement of United Way agencies, which are often asked to provide direct services to employees where they work. They are most successful when services and volunteer opportunities enhance but do not duplicate those provided by personnel divisions or organized labor.

We live our lives at a rapid pace. We tend to see only silhouettes rather than people of flesh and blood.

We have only quick glimpses of other people's joys and sorrows. Volunteering gives people a chance to enter other people's lives for more than a few seconds. It allows us to slow down and share in the experiences of others. People who have served their communities are compelling living proof of the power of volunteerism.

As the results come in, they show that when employees get involved in their community, they give more, and in far more substantial ways. Nearly 1,500 Kennewick, Washington, employees—the majority from companies with a year-round United Way presence—volunteered to work for United Way agencies

and other nonprofit organizations through United Way and the local Volunteer Center.

A United Way employee committee in Worcester, Massachusetts, encouraged United Way to help unemployed workers with information and placement services.

In Santa Barbara, over 100 Raytheon Company volunteers contributed time to thirty local agencies in 1985. A community service day was held, on which Raytheon volunteers tackled major construction and landscaping projects. Another group of Raytheon engineers altered an agency's computer so handicapped clients could use it.

More than 2,100 people were referred for services in 1984 as a result of the jointly offered United Way Sacramento Area/Central Labor Council's Information and Referral Agent Program (I-RAP). Sacramento's I-RAP program is the nucleus of its United Way at Work effort. Nearly 500 referral agents have been trained since 1980 and are at work in businesses, the federal and state governments, education, local unions and community agencies.

Through superlative cooperation between United Way and community health agencies, 25,000 Atlanta employees were screened for diabetes, blood pressure and colorectal cancer in 1985 at a United Way–sponsored health fair. Supporting literature, posters and exhibits reached 30,000 employees.

A summation of what United Way's increased presence at the workplace can bring comes from John Sullivan. John is United Way labor liaison for the United Way of Central Massachusetts, Worcester, and former president of United Steelworkers of America, local 3247. Explaining the United Way at Work idea to a company manager, John said:

> For the first time you'll be working with the union, not on grievances but on community problems. You're going to find out that union members aren't just interested in more money, but in a better community.
>
> And the union members will find out that you care what happens to your employees and their families.
>
> And then a great thing will happen. You'll develop such a good relationship that when you sit down to discuss a grievance, you'll focus on the issues and not on personalities, and that will make life a lot better for everybody.

We've discovered that if companies have seemed better at fostering community inside their walls than outside, its simply because they've lacked a mechanism that joins the two.

CHAPTER TWELVE

The American Mosaic

Today, there are more people of Irish ancestry in the United States than in Ireland; there are more Jews than in Israel, and more Blacks than in most African countries. New York has more than twice as many people of Polish descent than all but the largest cities in Poland.

Newcomers teem across our borders each year. They arrive from all points and settle wherever friends, or skills, or luck and chance take them. Occasionally, there is a large enough cultural contingent to form a town within a city. Miami has Little Havana, Baltimore has Little Italy, and Los Angeles has Koreatown.

There are now twenty-five cities in the nation with more than 50,000 Hispanic residents. Los Angeles has 2 million; Chicago has 422,000; Denver has 92,000; and Philadelphia has 63,000.

Whole nations live in America. There is no real majority anymore—only a mosaic of minorities.

A used-car dealer in Santa Ana, California, posts a sign saying, "We speak English." A sociologist found that a child at a certain Los Angeles school could hear forty-four different languages on the playground. Lance Morrow noted in a *Time* essay that a single cluster of stores in New York harbored a Korean beauty parlor, a Chinese watch store, a South Asian spice shop, a Chinese hardware store and a Korean barber.

But America is more than a mix of races. We are a mix of ages, of faiths, of incomes, of interests. We are a blend of blends.

A sense of community is what holds America together. When community exists, the individual feels that the world is playing fair, that the rules are not prejudiced and that everyone is welcome in the game.

Community implies closeness. Robert Nisbet has said it beautifully: "Community is a fusion of feeling and thought, of tradition and commitment, of membership and volition . . . Its archetype, both historically and symbolically, is the family."

Community is endangered when any one of the groups that comprise it is excluded. When groups of people are left out of society, they can become explosive, as when Miami erupted in the Liberty City riots or when the fifty-square-mile area of Watts was turned into a combat zone. Even a small excluded group can threaten the whole community.

Yet, the capability exists to build a system that serves the whole community. It begins with nonvested volunteer involvement. It demands long-term commitment to solving key social problems. It is based on the unwavering conviction that every community group should be invited to participate in the process, and that exclusion of even one key group is wrong. I have seen this problem-solving system in action. It is a marvelously successful mechanism.

CHAPTER THIRTEEN

Building Community: Three Case Studies

A river separates Lexington County and Richmond County in South Carolina. There is a bridge that allowed cars to travel from one county to the other, but for years there was no bridge for human concern. Years ago, the city folks of Columbia, in Richmond County, looked down on the "lint heads," or cotton mill workers, across the river. Neither group talked to the other. The river severed any sense of fellowship between the two.

United Way and its leadership in Columbia (I was then its chief professional officer) reached out to Lexington County. The most powerful man in Lexington County was the school superintendent. We gained his support and through it were able to help fund, up front, school lunch programs in the county. The United Way committed funds to Lexington County outright. Almost immediately after, Richmond County reached out.

After that first act of no-risk goodwill, a bridge of concern was built that led to a series of joint programs that, for the first time in memory, brought those two counties together to work as one trusting community.

By the mid-sixties, I had moved to Miami and helped form a broad community coalition there. It involved Dade County, the city of Miami Beach, the Dade County Public School System and the United Way. The board consisted of the mayors, top political leaders and top labor and business leadership in the area. An executive committee was also formed. On it was the head of the Chamber, the superintendent of schools, the chairman of the school board, the Dade County manager, and the Miami city manager. We met informally, at least every couple of weeks.

The coalition worked beautifully. We fought our fights, but in private. We negotiated behind the scenes.

We did most of our planning in informal sessions. Community problems were talked through. The attitude was to negotiate until we found a way to help. We parted company on occasion, but we worked to find a common ground that promoted the community's long-term interest. We trusted one another. We prevented many problems from ever bubbling up to the surface.

The school board asked our community coalition to study the public transportation system and to make recommendations on how to improve outreach to people in outlying areas. Bus service was not reaching black neighborhoods. Garbage collections were sporadic in poorer neighborhoods. The coalition found constructive solutions to these and other problems. We shored up the community a little.

The worst day in the history of South Bend, Indiana, was December 9, 1963: Black Monday. The president of Studebaker called a brief press conference in New York to say that the company's South Bend plant, which had been in operation for 111 years, would be closed.

A workforce of 8,700 was cut to 1,700, and even these were said to be temporary. All the flags in South Bend were flying at half mast to honor John F. Kennedy, who had been assassinated two weeks before. Ironically, Studebaker stock went up $.375 a share the day of the announcement.

As the chief professional officer of South Bend's United Way at the time, I was lamenting our financial loss. Needs would be greater and Studebaker represented a fifth of our giving base.

United Way's campaign chairman and I went to call on the chairman of the board of Studebaker, who was in the process of closing down the plant. This was before Black Monday, but even then the writing was on the wall. He said, "We obviously can't give you any money because we're closing down here; we're phasing in a new business."

Our campaign chairman seemed to agree. I asked if there was room for a dissenting view. I pointed out that the company was still paying taxes and electricity bills, that United Way was also a kind of public utility and that Studebaker was leaving us with people who had serious problems. United Way needed money to help, and we needed it now more than ever. It would be wrong to walk away from the responsibility for these people. The CEO agreed. He gave us a sizable corporate gift.

But then came the real catastrophe of the shut-

down—in effect, the end of an era. The Studebaker Brothers had begun building Conestoga wagons in South Bend in 1852. They built their first "horseless carriage" in 1902. Many of the workers who were laid off were the sons of Studebaker men. Some were the third generation at Studebaker, living in neighborhoods populated by other Studebaker families. Four thousand workers, average age fifty-four and a half, saw their whole support system dissolve. One weekend three unemployed workers killed themselves.

That weekend, I began thinking less about fundraising and more about these urgent needs. Here were thousands of workers without jobs. The Friday after the shutdown the *South Bend Tribune* carried eighteen more columns of help-wanted ads than the Friday before, but almost everything was for people with special skills. It must have crushed the hopes of assembly-line workers to look through them.

Right after the plant closed, thirty-five community leaders met to discuss ways to bring new business to South Bend to fill the Studebaker gap. The town's political and business leadership went to work on a package to help the city. Our chairman was then Congressman John Brademas, now president of New York University. He led a group to Washington to talk about immediate measures to help the unemployed. Out of the talk came $1 million to fund a job-training program. I remember writing on a cocktail napkin: "Ability Based on Long Experience." We called our program ABLE and came back to South Bend to put it to work.

United Way took the lead. We recruited union leaders and trained them as counselors. We recruited corporate executives to teach the older Studebaker workers how to handle themselves on interviews. Other volunteers went to work to find new job opportunities.

We learned a lot about getting people jobs. We

insisted that a volunteer go with each person who had a job interview, wait for them, and bring them home. We never let anyone go by themselves. No one felt they had to go through the process all alone. Through the leadership of Al Cooper, my successor in South Bend, Project ABLE placed 3,500 people in jobs over a three-year period.

CHAPTER FOURTEEN

The Community Table: The Ultimate Solution

Why did we get positive results in these instances—Columbia, Dade County and South Bend? Maybe it is better to look at what kept accomplishments from happening before United Way became involved.

For one thing, in Columbia particularly, labels got in the way: lint heads, city boys. Labels blocked the ability of groups to see each other as human beings. The by-product of efforts to bring people to a community table was that labels were lifted off. People saw each other as whole persons.

In all three cases, a community benefited from the auspices of a caring organization, neutral in every respect except about helping the entire community. In each case, United Way organized a forum; different

factions were brought together to try to define an issue and work out a solution. A community table was built.

This community table is like a floating poker game. It moves around. Issues change and the people you want to have at the table change. However, it is not an exclusive table. On any given issue, you assemble all the concerned parties—the people who can make a difference. They may be political rivals or competitors in the same business, but they agree on the priority of solving the issue at hand. And during the proceedings, there are no hidden agendas, just straight-up discussions of the issue.

The process must be disciplined, and there must be somebody to initiate and sustain it. United Way is not the only source of such initiative in a community: Sometimes United Way simply supports someone else's initiative.

The nuts and bolts are not difficult: You negotiate the definition of the problem, you negotiate the framework and scope of the problem, and you work to produce an action plan. You influence public policy if you have to. You do whatever is required, you take however long it takes to solve the problem.

What is often missing is a convenor—an independent, caring third force in society that lifts people above their vested interests, an agency willing to serve in a low-profile supporting role in the problem-solving process.

A continuum of unbiased concern is rare in our cities and towns. Uncomplicated as the theory of a community table is, it is rarely put into practice. In cities across America, people share the same roof and never talk to each other. Heads of organizations do not know each other. Politicians do not know each other. Leaders of one interest group do not know leaders of another.

But in this society, proud of its pluralism, we need a day-to-day process through which all a community's parts work together toward community goals. We need a framework that allows decision-makers to see the whole communal picture. We need to focus on the whole and not on fractious factions.

There is too little continuity of interest. Politicians' short terms in public office do not permit the long-term approaches that many problems require. For example, it will take at least a full generation to curb illiteracy. But we won't have a community apparatus through which key leaders can work steadily to eliminate illiteracy for maybe twenty years.

The benefits of getting people involved in commu-

nity problem-solving go far beyond getting problems solved. You build an ongoing capacity to deal with difficult issues. You build each participant's investment in the community. Key people are in position for long-term involvement in building community.

The need for a continuing forum—a free-form community table—is not a passing societal need. The more complicated our society becomes, the more necessary a neutral, caring instrumentality becomes. And the more necessary it becomes to involve business and labor leaders, politicians and representatives from the voluntary sector in the problem-solving process. And the more essential it becomes to involve a force such as United Way in the process, an organization that has the credibility and conscience to bring all the spokes of a community wheel together and make things start turning.

The Next Hundred Years

In 1931, after two years of history's worst depression, nearly half America's factories had closed their doors. President Hoover said we were "at the end of our string," and asked United Way's predecessor organization to help create a Committee on Mobilization for Human Needs.

We are not at the end of our string as a nation in 1987—not by a long shot. But there is a crisis of another sort. By almost any measure our sense of community has become badly eroded. And America may be in danger of becoming "just a place."

We feel thwarted and demoralized by the fact that a nation known for its great resources and ingenuity seems to be losing ground in the effort to build a decent, safe, caring society.

And we know now that it's not because people don't want to build better communities, but because of inadequate mechanisms through which they can help.

So we're beginning our second hundred years with another more hopeful and ambitious "mobilization for human needs." We're calling it the Second Century Initiative.

For openers, we're working to double our capacity to serve by doubling our volunteer and financial resources in the next five years. We are asking United Ways to review what needs they've met in the last five years, what their communities' needs will be in the next five and how they'll meet them.

That's not a modest goal—to increase United Way resources in the next five years as much as we've increased them in a hundred—but the needs of this nation make it a necessary and realistic one.

Corporate and employee volunteering and giving potential has only been scratched. In four years, giving from United Parcel Service employees rose from $400,000 to $8.7 million. In 1985, Pfizer's long-standing policy of matching its employees' United Way contributions paid off substantially. Donations ran 30 percent higher than the year before, resulting in 925,000 new corporate and employee dollars.

Since divestiture, AT&T corporate and employee gifts rose by $10.8 million. Sears Roebuck and Company and its employees raised almost $1 million in each of the past three years. IBM's corporate and employee gifts to United Way rose from $5 million to $26 million in seven years. Two years ago, there were no United Way campaigns in Walmart stores. Last year, Walmart employees gave $1 million.

Direct mail and other mass-marketing techniques are linking record numbers of volunteers to agencies.

United Ways are studying each other's volunteer involvement ideas as closely as they are one another's fund-raising strategies. For example, Memphis's United Way has received scores of requests for information about its well-planned volunteer program that reached 150,000 students of the Memphis city schools. I believe we are just beginning to learn how to raise money and mobilize volunteers.

There are already over 300 communities operating at a rate of growth that will double their financial resources by 1991. Can we raise that number to 600, or 900, or more? We can if we believe we can.

And if we invest money to back up that belief. It takes resources to increase resources. United Way will have to find the resources to expand its volunteer base, become involved in more community problem-solving ventures, fund new fund-raising mechanisms and step up its outreach to people in need. We've got to invest short-term resources in long-term growth.

But these resources are simply a means to the end of community building on a new scale.

Almost 40 percent of United Ways are already solving community problems through a community table, or coalition-building, approach. Results in the last few years have been unprecedented. Topeka, Kansas, was faced with a staggering number of children who had no one to come home to after school. United Way drew together a "latchkey" coalition of churches, social service agencies, city and school officials and parents. A series of programs have been started, all within walking distance of Topeka's grade schools.

In Fresno, California, the United Way organized a

coalition of agencies and seventy-three churches and synagogues to help feed those on the poverty margin.

In 1983, federal and state budget cuts eliminated many lower-income people from day care. United Way in Providence, Rhode Island, conducted a detailed study of day-care services in the area, which was shared with a coalition of child-care providers, legislators and the Governor's Block Grant Advisory Committee. All the lost child-care slots were restored.

James D. Robinson III, chairman and chief executive officer of American Express and current chairman of United Way's Board of Governors, believes deeply in United Way's potential. He has said, in fact, that if United Way were a corporation it would be ripe for takeover.

Richard J. Ferris, chairman, president, and chief executive officer of UAL, Inc., and United Way of America's chairman elect, is also chairman of the Second Century Initiative. Dick is helping United Way dream much bigger and do much more for this nation. New ground has been broken by another volunteer, John Akers, chairman of the board of IBM, who will follow Dick as chairman of United Way of America. Under John's leadership, United Way is becoming more sensitive to effective marketing strategies that will allow us to raise more money, recruit more volunteers and serve more people.

In 1987, our centennial year, through our Second Century Initiative, we're setting out to double our capacity in dollars and volunteers in the next five years. It is a bold recommitment to the spirit of caring that for a hundred years has helped United Way "bring out the best in all of us."

Second Century is an initiative of hope to a nation in need. Through it, and through the caring citizens of this country, America can become all we imagine she can be.

An Honor Roll of United Way Volunteers

BOARD OF GOVERNORS CHAIR	EXECUTIVE COMMITTEE CHAIR
1970 Bayard Ewing	1970 Harry T. Sealy
1971 Bayard Ewing	1971 M. M. Brisco
1972 Bayard Ewing	1972 M. M. Brisco
1973 James R. Kerr	1973 Laurence D. Bolling
1974 James R. Kerr	1974 Laurence D. Bolling
1975 C. Peter McColough	1975 Charles I. Stone
1976 C. Peter McColough	1976 Glenn E. Watts
1977 John W. Hanley	1977 Glenn E. Watts
1978 John W. Hanley	1978 Glenn E. Watts
1979 Clifton C. Garvin, Jr.	1979 J. C. Turner
1980 Clifton C. Garvin, Jr.	1980 J. C. Turner
1981 Donald V. Seibert	1981 Lisle C. Carter, Jr.
1982 Donald V. Seibert	1982 J. C. Turner and Lisle C.
1983 Robert A. Beck	Carter, Jr.
1984 Robert A. Beck	1983 Mary M. Gates
1985 James D. Robinson III	1984 Mary M. Gates
1986 James D. Robinson III	1985 Adele Hall
1987 Richard J. Ferris	1986 Adele Hall

The Agencies We Serve

Twenty-two hundred United Way organizations fund an estimated 37,000 health and social service agencies across the nation. The following two lists illustrate the types of health and social service providers that participate in United Ways' allocations process. Group I lists national agencies and affiliates which receive funding from United Ways. Group II provides a *sample* of local agencies that also receive funding from United Ways. But numerous other health and welfare organizations also receive United Way funding.

GROUP I: NATIONAL AGENCIES AND MAJOR NAME AGENCIES

Agencies for the Aged
Agencies for the Blind
American Cancer Society*
American Diabetes Association
American Heart Association*
American Red Cross
American Social Health Association
Arthritis Foundation
Association for Retarded Citizens
Big Brothers/Big Sisters
Boys Clubs
Boy Scouts
Camp Fire, Inc.
Catholic Charities
Cerebral Palsy Associations
Child Welfare League
Council on Social Work Education
Easter Seal Societies
Epilepsy Foundation of America
Family Service Association
Girls Clubs
Girl Scouts
Goodwill Industries
Hearing and Speech Centers
Heart Associations
Homemaker—Home Health
    Service
Hospitals
Jewish Federations

Jewish Community Centers and
    YM/YWHAs
Mental Health Associations
National Council on Alcoholism
National Council on Crime and
    Delinquency
National Cystic Fibrosis Research
    Foundation
National Hemophilia Foundation
National Multiple Sclerosis Society
National Recreation and Park
    Association
Neighborhood Centers and
    Settlement Houses
Salvation Army
Travelers Aid Association
United Cancer Council, Inc.
United Seamen's Services
United Service Organizations
    (USO)—Local and National
United Way Planning Organizations
Urban League
Visiting Nurse Associations
Volunteer Bureaus and Voluntary
    Action Centers
Volunteers of America
Young Men's Christian Association
Young Women's Christian
    Association

*In several cities, the American Cancer Society and American Heart Association receive support from the United Way campaign.

GROUP II: LOCAL SERVICE AGENCIES

Health Services

Berkeley Women's Health
    Collective
Chicano Community Health Center
Child Haven
Expectant Parent

Hale Ho-ola Hou (Walk-in Clinic)
Indian-Chicano Health Center
School Children's Health Care
Well Baby Clinic

Provision for Emergencies and Basic Needs

Dial-A-Ride
Children's Milk Fund
Christmas Fund for Children
Community Pantry
Dinners for Shut-Ins
Emergency Assistance Fund
Emergency Fuel & Life Support
Emergency Resource Bank

Friends in Service Helping
Helena Indian Alliance
Hunger Task Force
Mutual Help Center
Western Neighbors
Youth Emergency Fund
Free Stores, Inc.

Multipurpose Social and Cultural Services

Albany Inter-Racial Council
Centro de la Comunidad Unida
Chinatown Service Center
Country Neighbor Program
Hispanic Affairs & Resource Center
Intertribal Friendship House

Japanese American Service
    Committtee
Korean Community Service Center
Mi Casa Resource Center for
    Women
Suburban Community Services

Child and Youth Services

Filipino Youth Activities
Horizons Summer Program
Inner City Youth League
Iowa Runaway Service
Juvenile Court Volunteers
Los Niños Center
New Directions for Young Women
Operation Getting It Together
Puerto Rico Youth Development
Tiny Tots
Umoja Extended Family
Volunteers for Youth
Youth Activities Council
Youth Line

Neighborhood Services

All Nations Neighborhood Center
American Indian Center, Inc.
Casa de Amigos
Centers for New Horizons
Centro Cultural Chicano
Chinese American Civic Association
Consolidated Neighborhood
  Services
House of Neighborly Service
Karamu House
Polish Community Center
Village Visiting Neighbors

Special Services for Women

A Woman's Place
Advocates for Battered Women
Casa de Esperanza
Center for Women in Transition
Women Organized Against Rape
Women's Resource Center
Family Tree, Inc.
My Sister's House
New Beginnings
Spouse Abuse Shelter Project
Women Helping Women

ACKNOWLEDGMENTS

Before there was a book, there was Tom Hallin—volunteer, business leader, friend—who convinced me to sit still long enough to begin this project. When I first came to United Way of America in 1970, I said, "Tom, I need your help." His wise guidance and counsel have been a source of strength and comfort to me ever since.

This book began as a stack of bite-size tapes that were transcribed one sleepless week by Rina Duncan, Terry Colley and Barbara Florence. Their patience has held up through many revisions for which I am grateful.

I owe thanks also to my long time associate, John Glaser, who helped in dozens of ways; to Dick Cornuelle, who served as key advisor, editor and strategist; and to Dee Morgan who so ably assisted in the project in its earliest stages. Peter Chandler took my words and made them better.

I reserve special tribute to that genius Gil Meekins, a wonderfully creative human being and a magnificent person, whose illustrations warm every chapter.

I am blessed to work with an extraordinary group at United Way of America, led by Dick O'Brien. Many of them reviewed drafts of this book and contributed research to it. You have my deep appreciation.

It has been my great privilege to serve the people

of this nation through United Way. I am deeply indebted to my fellow United Way professionals and to the many dedicated volunteers with whom I have the joy of working. They continue to propel United Way from one plateau of service to another.